Reading Champion

That's Not My Teddy

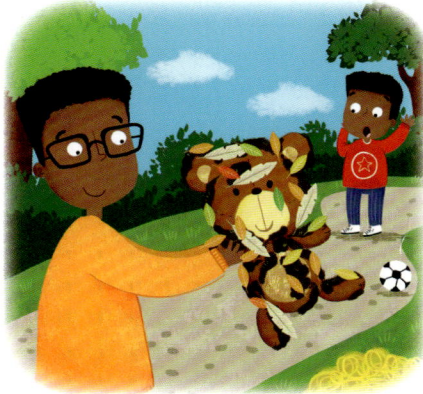

by Damian Harvey and Angelika Skudamore

W

FRANKLIN WATTS

LONDON•SYDNEY

Dad and Adi went to the park.
"Come on, Teddy," said Adi.

Adi went on the swing.
"Come on, Teddy," said Adi.

Teddy went into the puddle.
"Oh no!" said Dad.

Adi went on the slide.

"Come on, Teddy," said Adi.

Teddy went into the leaves.
"Oh no!" said Dad.

"Where is Teddy?" said Adi.

"Here he is," said Dad.

Adi looked at Teddy.
"That's not my Teddy,"
said Adi.

15

Dad put Teddy in the wash.

"Come on, Teddy," said Adi.

"That's my Teddy," said Adi.

18

Story trail

Start

Start at the beginning of the story trail. Ask your child to retell the story in their own words, pointing to each picture in turn to recall the sequence of events.

Independent Reading

This series is designed to provide an opportunity for your child to read on their own. These notes are written for you to help your child choose a book and to read it independently.

In school, your child's teacher will often be using reading books that have been banded to support the process of learning to read.

Use the book band colour your child is reading in school to help you make a good choice. *That's Not My Teddy* is a good choice for children reading at Yellow Band in their classroom to read independently.

The aim of independent reading is to read this book with ease, so that your child enjoys the story and relates it to their own experiences.

About the book

Adi and Dad visit the park with Adi's favourite teddy. While Adi plays in the playground, Teddy takes a few tumbles and becomes very dirty, so Adi doesn't recognise it. Luckily Dad knows what to do – a wash will make Teddy good as new.

Before reading

Help your child to learn how to make good choices by asking: "Why did you choose this book? Why do you think you will enjoy it?" Look at the cover together and ask: "What do you think the story will be about?" Support your child to think of what they already know about the story context. Read the title aloud and ask: "What do you think has happened to Teddy? Why do you think that?" Remind your child that they can try to sound out the letters to make a word if they get stuck.

Decide together whether your child will read the story independently or read it aloud to you. When books are short, as at Yellow Band, your child may wish to do both!

During reading

If reading aloud, support your child if they hesitate or ask for help by telling the word. Remind your child of what they know and what they can do independently.

If reading to themselves, remind your child that they can come and ask for your help if stuck.

After reading

Support comprehension by asking your child to tell you about the story. Use the story trail to encourage your child to retell the story in the right sequence, in their own words.

Help your child think about the messages in the book that go beyond the story and ask: "Do you think Adi knows what has happened to Teddy? Why / why not?" Give your child a chance to respond to the story: "Did you have a favourite part? Have you got a favourite toy or belonging? Where would you take it?"

Extending learning

Help your child understand the story structure by using the same sentence patterns and adding some new elements. "Let's make up a new story about a toy bunny. Becca went on the roundabout. 'Come on, Bunny,' said Becca. 'Oh no! Where is Bunny?' Now you try. What will happen to Bunny in your story?

Your child's teacher will be talking about punctuation at Yellow Band. On a few of the pages, check your child can recognise capital letters, question marks, exclamation marks and full stops by asking them to point these out.

Franklin Watts
First published in Great Britain in 2023
by Hodder and Stoughton

Copyright © Hodder and Stoughton Ltd, 2023
All rights reserved.

Series Editors: Jackie Hamley and Melanie Palmer
Series Advisors: Dr Sue Bodman and Glen Franklin
Series Designers: Cathryn Gilbert and Peter Scoulding

A CIP catalogue record for this book is
available from the British Library.

ISBN 978 1 4451 7684 0 (hbk)
ISBN 978 1 4451 7686 4 (pbk)
ISBN 978 1 4451 8777 8 (ebook)

Printed in China

Franklin Watts
An imprint of
Hachette Children's Group
Part of Hodder and Stoughton
Carmelite House
50 Victoria Embankment
London EC4Y 0DZ

An Hachette UK Company
www.hachette.co.uk

www.reading-champion.co.uk

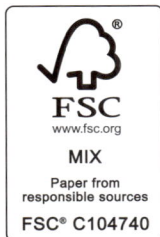

FSC
www.fsc.org
MIX
Paper from
responsible sources
FSC® C104740